Voices from Kibuli Country

poems

Dannabang Kuwabong

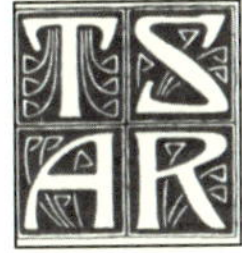

We acknowledge the support of the Canada Council for the Arts for our publishing program. We also acknowledge support from the Government of Ontario through the Ontario Arts Council.

We acknowledge the financial support of the Government of Canada through the Canada Book Fund for our publishing activities.

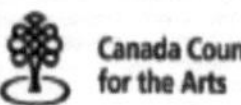

Canada

Cover design by Peggy Stockdale
Cover image: Abdolhamid Ebrahimi / iStockphoto

Library and Archives Canada Cataloguing in Publication

Kuwabong, Dannabang, 1955-, author
Voices from Kibuli country : poems / Dannabang Kuwabong.

ISBN 978-1-927494-28-8 (pbk.)

I. Title.

PS8571.U89V65 2013 C811'.54 C2013-904881-2

Printed and bound in Canada by Coach House Printing

TSAR Publications
P. O. Box 6996, Station A
Toronto, Ontario M5W 1X7
Canada
www.tsarbooks.com

Contents

I. Those Who Step into Shadows

The Signposts

Tuesday
day of tears arrives
those of laughter
hang whimpering
on mourning lips

Wednesday
love
false divinity
wasp sting of desire
mirage above
jagged rocks

Thursday
hands stretch for touch
mirage slithers away
into dunes
lily in sands

Friday
wail sob wail
mire of emotions
my soul sails aimless
fortune of sorrow

Saturday
she waits at crossroads
devout devotee of misery
smiles at my screams

Sunday
somehow a blade stands
shimmering grass at flood's rim
The story of Pestle
solitude's hope

Monday
skilfully masked wound
oozing rot
attracts blue flies
cloaking scream of life

New Year's Eve

It is winter once again on New Year's Eve
Memories of our hooded selves rise up
Silhouettes striding against neon horizons
Gloved hand in gloved hand careless of the cold
We lean on each other's breaths for warmth
And walk slowly to La Luna on Hess Street
Hungry for crispy cold salad and sweaty Labatt

We always found a spot avoiding conspicuousness
Chilling out with smooth blues and jazz or roots reggae
Then I would recall to you our days in Lebanon
Fresh from military academy in Tamale
Sent to keep the peace between the cross and the crescent
Gazing desiring but unable to love until now

Our mates from other Black Star regiments
Spent their dreams collecting durables of consumption
Trophies of their journeys to foreign lands
We saved our dreams in our wallets to purchase our escape
When news came of coups and counter-coups
Of executions and vendettas in our beloved Ghana
To this land then of great promise to those who would endure
To Canada then we came running on paper clips of terror

Welcome to Canada/Bienvenue au Canada
To Hamilton then a steel city we came with hope
Me as a car-park attendant and security man at Henderson
You as janitor at Juravinski Innovation Tower at St Joe's
We found refuge in a basement on Wilson Street North
Windowless but better than home we told ourselves
Now without job or status and out in these cold streets
And you gone your own way and I to mine

Often then on every New Year's Eve
I saunter to this spot between Main West and King West
Where Hess Runs toward York Street
I stand facing La Luna sighing for your touch
Nodding my head without ever hearing
Those soft trombones and saxophones that soothed us
Coming through the cracks of the Jazz Club
And I wish for a sip of Typhoo or a cappuccino

All that is gone now only the shadowy memories remain
They fade daily and with each cold winter night
I walk over to the dim-lit Lazy Flamingo Bar
The ladies dance Canadian flamingo for me
The ladies smile sweetly and wink at me
But I do not notice their piercing eyes of desire
I sip Molson without passion and watch the lights flicker
And wish I could once more gaze into your eyes

Oh! For one more New Year's Eve with you in my arms!
Under these willow trees on Lovers Lane in Ancaster.

Triple Rainbow

We plant our feet
My daughters and I
In the parking lot of Westcliff Mall
Undeterred by the fall drizzle
We watch ecstatically
Glorious triple rainbows
Define Hamilton's smoky downtown

The sheer beauty of those competing rainbows
We say to ourselves
Portends no ill-will to us
Perhaps, we say auspiciously
The Virgin Mary will appear to us too
We who are faithful to her call
Just coming from Mass that Saturday
From Regina Mundi Catholic Church

So we stand with shimmering smiles
Gazing with expectant faces
Circled by bemused shoppers
Soaking in the wonder of nature
Soaking in the fumes of progress

Suddenly from East Mountain
We witness a flock of silvery wings
Gliding, glittering, shining, shimmering
Towards us
This must be Angel Gabriel we think
Coming to announce the Virgin's coming
Behind us to the South Mountain
A globe of yellow pierce the darkening sky
Shatters into a kaleidoscope

And lightning dances to the rhythm of thunder
Across the Western horizon

We still stand
Joined by other believers
The silvery wings pass
Only seagulls escaping to Florida
Carrying our miracle of rainbows with them
Every day now I stop by the spot
I look up and pray
For the return of my triple treat
While standing in the rain
On Mohawk West and Upper Paradise
By the Church of Regina Mundi
Awaiting the day of interrogation on Concession Street

Interrogation on Concession Street

They come up
Quietly smiling

Sudden from shadows of their history
Offering sympathy in word platters
To ease burdens of guilt
Under my stranded dance step

They come up
Winking

I am interrogated casually
About origins of my smile
My response designed to obstruct
Become confirmations of their dreams
That I must taste of defeat

They leave grinning through shadows on Concession Street
And I standing, confounded in the silence of fear

Exorcizing Nostalgia

For those Ghanaians in the diaspora living on the margins of nostalgia
Food is our ritual weapon of our restoration

I have seen our numbers swell in winter marches through sludge
Carrying our bags of desire toward allocated dens of hope

We are the motley crowd of diverse faiths in remembered tastes
Thus we bond our dreams in these tiny temples of familiar smells

Their names are listed in the Hamilton handbook as grocery stores
We of the confused minds call them our temples of remembrance

To Rama Tropical Foods lining James Street North and Murray Street West
To Mama Africa on Canon East and Ashley Street North

To Lyn's Linstead Market on Upper Gage and other unregistered tropical foods
We come carrying our empty stomachs seeking fulfillment of our dreams

Like the smells of attraction we swarm around the shelves of our daily bread
Where balls of *kenkey,* balls of *dokuno,* Ga and Fante or Jamaican steamed

Like blue flies the smell of goat and cow, the smell of sheep and chicken too
The stink of fish, fresh or smoked, salted or frozen blends with cow guts too

Draw us all one and all the faithful lost to find our way back home
We saunter in genuflecting in perfect poise of repentance

Our expectant faces survey the ingredients for our purification
Our panting souls yearning for the moment of sanctification

Here on the centre shelves of the alters sacks of *garden eggs*
Bruised and battered better gifts for our sinful acts of departures

Beside them sprawl hairy yummy yams and coco-yams from Ghana
Conversing with sweet potatoes and plantains on the beauty of a coconut

Around them my brethren and *sistren* with collective guilt of conscience
Congregate to sing praises to the various shapes and smells of fish

This first phase of public confession done we turn to the prayers of the faithful
Requesting bulging prayers of *fufu* flour and pounded yam flour in their bagful

We offer prayers for the bags of bean and millet flour, corn and cassava flour
We search our consciences for plantain and Tom Brown flour, *kokoo* and *banku* flour

Our gift offering to the gods of nostalgia demands the presence of *Zomi* palm oil
To light the candles of peace we must also include in the offering basket coconut oil

The ritual demands an anointing thus we seek the oil from the shea nut
And for soup the gods like the most, we must include butter of peanut

Lest we get blasted to eternal hell of nostalgia *egusi, neri,* and bitter leaf are good
Cassava and pepper leaves, battered cans of *calalloo, aleefu or nkontomire* too

We move one by all to the sanctuary of smells where the high
priest wields a cleaver
Hacking and bagging portions of the unblemished scapeguts of
goat, cow and chicken

We squeeze the squishy bags of guts and after cup our perfumed
palms to our faces
Breathe in the breath of eternal forgiveness and place orders with
expectation of graces

We shift into patterns of hierarchies of holiness according to
heads, guts and feet
Those of snapper, herring, and mackerel meet those who seek
kpanla and crayfish greet

We all one and sundry receive our desired bags of absolution and
penance
We roll forward to receive our paid benedictions at the counter of
pennies

But some cannot receive the benediction without the sting of
pepper sauce
Powder alone is not enough to burnout the hidden sin behind
the wisdom teeth

Salvation, my *sistren* and brethren, shouts the priest's assistant in
faith
Does not come by bread alone but you must wash with the sponge
of faith

Thus we each grab our fishing nets to catch the dirt of our sinful flesh
Rubbed with *kotokoli* and steamed in the waters of purification

Our service is over now and we go in peace to serve our needs
At the door we grab bulletins of our nations and music cds

To sustain the growth of our faith we seize pirate copies of *Nollywood*
We say we need these movies to fight nostalgia through *Ghollywood*

Thus forgiven and blessed
We retreat to our hideouts chattering alleluias in tongues:
Preis bi bikos naw naw awa beli dem go don ful wel wel
Eni katakata for Afrika den go de run komot kariim palava go
And wi no go de tink sey wi no de for Gana or Nijeriya tu nko
So derfor wi no go get eni problem egen for wan wik for os
Na im wi go de nyam plenti plenti chop so te beli kom wan berst
And wi go de jos slip beta slip kpatakpata.

Thus while walking with our blessings home, they can come up smiling
Sputtering their interrogations of my origins on Concession Street

Shadows on Concession Street

peace to the world
goodwill to all

when the fall of tears arrive
only those shed by our laughter
will chant down, quivering
on the lips of our dementia

then against the annual poles
erected to hold the annual crib
where a plastic baby annually lies
clawing at freezing winds

we gather around the rickety shed
all around the square anxious faces
stump around with frozen smiles
speaking to a frightened deer

in the shadow of their erected peace
will the flashes of revolving wrath
sustained by their dying desires
glimmer like neons in our memory?

peace to the world
goodwill to all

will we the tormented be entangled
within their chippings of peace
to sunshine the shades of our years to come?

peace to the world
goodwill to all
who step into shadow

will the smolders of present pain
become ashes beneath these gasps
soothe these shivering withdrawals?

for the illusions of betrayals
have coursed through our arteries
hardened our heart strings

what jingles then can charm
with breathless supplications
these flashes of a reckoning?

what candle can rekindle passion
what stories can restore reason
to cold debates on hasty actions?

we who are lured by lurid visions
through cellophane screens
in midnight their secret dens

believing we could erase the heart prints
where no eye can perceive
when reckoning rises flashing

forgotten finger contours
what shadows can shield
our disgrace beyond reckoning

peace to the world
goodwill to all
who step into the shadow

where then to cover our eyes
from this glare on our souls?

we who shoo away

the oracles of peace
now beat our scrawny ribs
now embrace dying lies
godheads of our youth

we retreat toward West Mountain
toward St Joseph's and Henderson
looking for our Marian Wing
looking for our prisons of hope

the horizon recedes
the horizon recedes
yet looms above Mountain Brow
as we trudge through cold mist

where then to cover our eyes
from this glare on our souls?

through our vacant pupils we wonder:

is there a way then
to re-member our dis-mem-ber-ing
is there a way to un-ripe
our pre-mature rot-ting
our fruits of un-knowing?

is this dreaded darkness then
is this tunnel on Younge Street
a canal to a lost tomorrow
splattered and squandered
on a mirage of selfhood?

through our vacant pupils we wonder:

when to have been
was not to have been?

in Whitehall they snort over our poems:
the fall of fears.

only these shed by our laughter
chant down, quivering
on the sound of our dementia

we are the yellowing leaves of fall
we boasted our beauty before death
we boasted before we gained the glory

the glorious luster of green
now flattens on a rock of moss
awaiting the northern gust

to mulch us on the path to humus
where our story
may nourish new roots
new births and desires.

we hear the siren: we huddle we huddle, we lie peaceful on white stretchers, beneath white sheets, surrounded by hands in white mittens, needled and corded, chloroform coded we sing Te Deums, there is no chlorophyll on a sunless day, breathing suspended, we suspended from the ceiling, we look down whispering:

blood is the trial!
peace to the world
blood is the trial!
goodwill to all
blood is the trial!!
who step into shadow
only blood is the trail!

Those Who Step into Shadows

Somewhere in these places of Hamilton and Niagara:
Niagara-on-the-Lake, Angel Inn, The Royal Connaught Hotel,
The Right House, St Paul's Church, Hamilton Place, White-
hern, Hermitage Ruins, Lovers Lane, Customs House.

The headless horseman rides always in haste
Behind him the lady in white with hair flowing in the wind
They ride across the sky of Hamilton and Niagara Regions
Carrying their frozen passion over these unwary crowds

I have seen them often on New Year's Eve from Mountain Brow
The lady in white leading the poor and homeless
On top the roof of the Royal Connaught now Holiday Inn
To hurl themselves from the parapet restaurants
And dance before the rich in splashes of blood
As they sink their tobacco stained teeth into rare sirloins

I have seen all this because I am the man
With the white bedsheet around my neck
Dangling from a closet bar for clothes
Legs kicking desperately to gain floor hold
Quivering to a whimpering stop
Waiting for my maiden in white to rescue my limp body

I have seen it all with my gaping eyes
Hiding behind the shadows of these woods
Where the still air rises to rustle the grass
And stifled lamentations of rejected love
Announces the advent of Mary's ghost
Searching for Black under the willow tree

I who has eyes only for the dead have seen them all
I have heard the language of love turned to blood
My Ives, my Canada, how have I loved thee
But Otto built a wall of violence over us
Oh my dark lady in the Customs House
Stranded in Lovers Lane waiting for her coachman

I have made my vespers at St Paul's on James South
I am at the Carriage House and I come to you
Floating at the end of a rope from a rafter
Oh Mary of wilted dreams on Lovers Lane
In this state of tightened larynx I forget the songs of love
But from now on our corpses shall shine by night
Our passions shall glow at the Sulphur Springs
Giving healing to those betrayed by sickness of love

For blood is my trial

Blood Is the Trial

so says this silent stiff body:
for my hands have strayed
and now lie bodiless
from the statue of my desire

deep night to deep night
i waited on each theme
deep night through deep night
careful to click the blank screen

where my ears assembled
the faintest trace of steps

i, dreamed in this cauldron of deceit
i, wove tales of extreme success
i, trained bloodshot gaze of difference
to a belief that they could not see

but somewhere I knew they knew
yet my raison d'être cocooned
in the ire of my rejection
of what we all had dreamed

i fired invectives
i shut them down
i pushed them out

pushed them out with ear blocks
pushed them out with loud talk
pushed them out with great sulk

their words of revelation
i smashed with determination

their noises of inspiration
i choked with determination

arguments for moderation
i debunked with determination
i preferred my chaos
i refused their order
i foamed if caught

i kept still if sought
i shut myself behind silence
till my blood frothed through all openings
now these fingers begin to bleed
now these fingers make bloody scrawls
on these black papery beads

stuck on the illusions of images
i hear their gentle calls of my name
their fingers sooth my bursting brow

the vision flickers and is gone
through these circuits hidden in a mouse
i hear the pounding in the head

numb knuckles
crack of knees
snap of spine
flash of razor
Darkness!

blood is the trial
tell the rest awhile.

The scream of Life

Out of the darkness of red waters
The scream of life
The shriek for light
The waters do not choke
The water gates open
To the push of fright
The prairies succumb to the touch of light
And the heat of infant flesh
Secures comfort in maternal folds

Thus I sprawl
Beneath the maple tree
Amnesia beckoning to my fear
What next to do
When neither hate nor love is present?
Words of doubt
Thoughts of oblivion
Sounds of doom
Begin the desire ritual for vision

Power: it is not in us to create
Power: it is not in us to transform
Power: it is not in us to donate
Power: it is not in us to transcend
Power to withhold all these
Awakens the genii of fear in the supplicant
Only limitation imposed by dreams
Sits watching sits watching.

Dawn of My Death 1

at the dawn of my dying
my requiem refused orations
my marble grave sang its own praises
to honor caves of leaves
planning how to feed themselves
to the gnarled roots of maple
that give birth to them

at the dawn of my death
my tombstones walked away
slowly into the boiling west
rushing across the bilious Niagara Falls
that rushes toward Lake Ontario
rushes across Lake Erie
rushes to the Grand River
where the Sanqueen and Rideau
become the Devil's Punchbowl

at the dance of my death
the cantors speak only of silence
draw shadows before memory
where all language is a great grunt
what then? what then?
to do with a body suspended
on this day between dusk and dawn
where the grave shall be no nest
where the task refuses a stone
where soil rises beyond the ground

on the dawn of my death
my closed eyes open new doors
to The emptiness to The fullness.

Dawn of My Voice

"Je suis un souvenir qui n'atteint pas le seuil"

Aimé Césaire, "Le griffon"

But grandpa in this land surrounded
I refuse to be that memory
That evacuated brainwave
Caught between the final footfall
And the drag of ancient chains
Gazing without entering
Into the shadows of the threshold of voice

I understand your meaning
I drink in your empty stare
But caught in these withering reeds
I become the whistling wind
That rustles the dry blades of grass
That shakes down the green leaves

In this forest of flirting shadows
I am the very memory lodged in their memory of forgetting
I recall my birth pangs at the threshold
That entice their gazes
Causes them to miss their steps
Straying them in circles of songs
On the backyard of remembrances

I am their purgatory in conception
Parce que je suis un souvenir qui atteint le seuil

Dawn of My Dying 1

Let the genes of Mwaakpieong arise
In these lands of frozen breath
Behind broken walls on James South
A figure wails at midnight
To the tunes of unheard xylophones:

"If dying is like lying
Then my journey with you
Is a stranded dance
Where the drums have ceased
Syncopation now a monotone
Only the echoes fade away
Wavering over the wet goat skin

"My fingers no longer arouse their rhythmic pride
For the fingers that dare
Only blood drops are the answer
Only the moan of the *korinjong* of Konyeleh
Still strides the night on Mountain Brow

"I alone simmer in the cauldron of my silence
Suspicion as my suspended gaoler
Cross-checks every word fashioned
In the breath of my panic of thinking
I who is molded by invisible voices
Into these notes of assured betrayals

Then they say through clenched teeth
Love is an eternity of lightning compassion
How then to conjure an angle of satisfaction
Into this eternity of emptiness

I who am stranded here between teardrops and screams
Sweet darkness engulfing my hot heart of pain

Night of Reckoning

this is the night of fore-dreams
soon all entrances will be sealed
soon all exit doors will be concealed

security thighs plant astride
block the push from within
block the pull from without

soon I sit alone in my darkness
soon all lights will blink and die
watching these stranded pulses

I will hand out coupons of love
I who dreamed of rivers of love
never received a half cup of love

I will hand out tickets to love
I who never dreamed enough
must give a full cup of hate

until this dry and shrived gourd
in the back lanes of Hamilton
as the fortunate pass by me

hunched beside a brick wall
hugging the cold concrete
as the fortunate veer away

This is the night of fore-dreams
Soon all entrances will be sealed
Soon all exit doors will be concealed

soon I sit alone in my darkness
soon all lights will blink and die
watching these stranded pulses

I have verified my ventricles
Courted my cerebellum
Tempted my temporal

I have browsed my brain stem
occupied my occipital
pried through my parietal

Confronted my frontal
This is the night of fore-dreams
Soon all entrances will be sealed

but nothing left nothing left
soon I sit alone in my darkness
soon all exit doors will be concealed

perchance in all this there is a now
I must take no more hints

perchance in all this there is glimmer
I must assume no more goals

for in this foreday morning
all lights will blink and die
in this night of fore-dreams
when all entrances will be sealed
when all exits will be concealed
I will remember the songs of yore to my Duma

Approaching Athens, Ohio

in this town of corrugated brainwaves
you must know your paths
a false turn and step
you could be nowhere
below the shadows of the Appalachians

observe though how the Horking River
runs in brown circles
hugging the limestone of the Appalachians,
looking for entry to the Ohio.

were I the waters of the Horking
my frustrated moves would be wilder
as I meander looking for escape
blocked and mined at every turn
below the tail ends of the Appalachians

yet I am not it
for it seems happy in its flow
puffing up here and there
squeezing through undergrowths
between creeks lining the Appalachians

I wonder why it begins here
In the center of Canal Town
erupting from tiny cracks
in the only flat lands
sprawled beneath the Appalachians

but my wonder is just a wonder
for my memory returns to Athens

where Court Street like a spinal cord
holds the city's nerves in check
hugging the lungs of the city
ending below shadows of the Appalachians

Athens Penetrated

Athens not of Greece but of Ohio squats drowsing
In the nether ends of the Appalachians
There is a sense of calm abandon
As we drive through its major street
From nerve-tense Columbus

I notice the air breathes cleaner
I sense the people smile better
As our GPS lady commands
Turn right, turn right now
Then recalculating and silence
We arrive by error at Baymont Inn and Suites
Destination 20 Home Street

In a minute I check in and drop my tote bag
Leave for Baker Center at Ohio University

Our sense of wonder
How this tiny town
Accommodates our differing desires
And yet maintains its calm

Our sense of wonder and wander
Over the globed domes and spiral gables
The brief roundabout in the city center
The fake Appian way of cobblestones
The sudden shortage of what the city promises

Distances here
Are measured in hyperboles
We ask how far to Baker Hall

From China King Restaurant
About a mile says the guide
So we prepare for a long walk of five minutes
Pericles' ghost welcomes us to Baker Hall.

Woman Waiting at Charlotte Airport

Was it that time of year of neither winter nor spring
When hope for warmth is the only stirring in the heart
As the woman dressed in white awaited her hour hope
That at any tick of the seconds' hand he would appear
Dragging his multicoloured suitcase after him
Stepping briskly with that broad grin of his
That parts the grays from the browns above his lips
And uncovers those coffee-stained teeth so uneven
Yet she loved him and waited for him with sighs

I watched her from behind my squinted eyes
Every now and then she looked at her watch
Her tired eyelids tried to cover her panic-seized eyes
Prying through the frost-glazed glass of the terminal
Praying that every B767 taxiing in was from Dallas
No not yet, for this one was from Toronto
She watched the passengers like escaping prisoners
Rush out from the tunnels of arrival, dragging multicoloured bags
Disappearing into tunnels of departures, but where was her cowboy?

Her drooping eyelids lit up again
As a garbled voice over the PA announced
The arrival of a US Airways B767 from Dallas
Perhaps her cowboy would finally descend from this Pegasus
She rose briskly and pushed her hair from her face
Refit her dress and checked her teeth against the mirrored glass
She walked up, she walked down, and she turned around watching
Waiting for the yodel from her cowboy in plaited boots
She was waiting and hoping, her face beginning to sag

I watched her now without blinking from my anxiety to know

For soon like a startled cobra she stretched her neck
Peered into the now depleted tunnel of new arrivals
There were no more squeaky crunches announcing other faces

She slumped on the seat in front of the mounted TV
The news flash from CNN confronted her directly
"An American citizen of suspected New Mexican heritage
Has been deported to Mexico under the Undocumented Alien's Act"

Of what other crime, we are not told, but his names became his status:
Gilberto Anabaptist Schmidt Roberto Alberto
Could not prove citizenship of New Mexico for a Hispanic
For if from New Mexico then Hispanic and hence Mexican

He failed to speak in plain American where he comes from
He failed to explain in American where he was going
He failed to convince in American his preferred decision
To marry an all American virgin called Charlotte in Charlotte

"He fit the profiles of UAs in our folios of profiles
We had no choice but apply the law without prejudice."
She blinked tears as a silent scream escaped her quivering lips
In the horizon the yellow sun slunk behind Tucson Mountains

I joined the queue to board my plane to Puerto Rico, wondering!

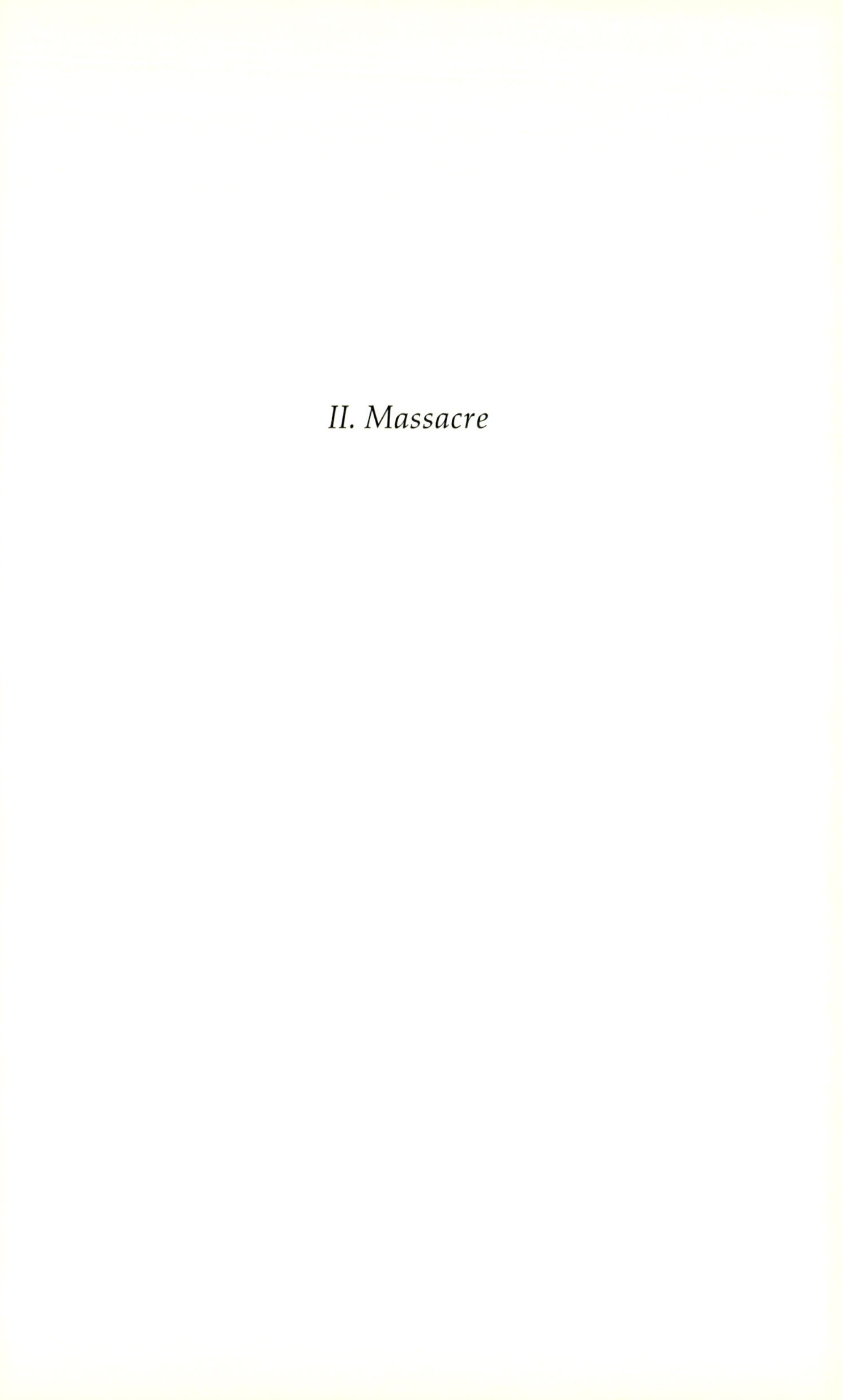

II. Massacre

While listening to Kwame Dawes speak of healing poetry—Day 1

For those who travel together and moan together with passion
The spiritual is the magic of their experience of grounding
The simpatico of their understanding bonds their pain
With energies of unity in their journeys of artistic resurrections
Thus we too are witnesses to post-Katrina Louisiana
And we too are witnesses to post-earthquake Haiti
And we too are witnesses to post-tsunami Japan

We must therefore sing testimonies of these concrete rubbles
Of sudden tombstones and the newly buried without benedictions
To these ports of crushed bones hither we come
Not with rosary beads of tears but with maracas of song
We come with seeing eyes not to look but to listen
To these children still flying kites on nature's dung hills
Where detached fingers stick through crevices defying death

We too come to listen to our own fears of understanding
What moves the ring finger not yet calloused or crushed
But rises in graffiti hope along the broken backs of walls
We too have come to collect the tears that refuse to drop
We seek comfort in the daughter holding the head of a mother
While the brother drops under a hail of shattering bricks
We who wish to travel with their energies of love have seen

We have seen the unity of their footfalls and hopes
Of these children of Africa born in the Caribbean
Those who survived death by drowning, those who survived death
by whiplash
These who have lived in the shadows of their laughter
Opening sealed doors of their hearts sans suspicion

Of those who now huddle in secret chambers of reflection
Listening to the rhythms of their drumbeats of pain

They welcome us who have come seeking our own redemption rains
The good and the bad, the ugly and the weird, behind mount hope
See us stepping through these dust clouds of after-quake
Sifting through these broken slabs of fallen futures
And Gantier, Gantier the mother of mothers, says Kwame
Sits propping all the tombs of the brave in her head
Blessing all who dare to come with their own agendas

Day 2: Listening to Kwame Dawes speak about his interview with a woman in Haiti

In her secret chambers where we met her she said:
"they think I sell beer in this broken shack of mine
so when you depart from here
you must be seen clutching bottles of beer"
in other words we must move surreptitiously
step gingerly through these catacombs of despair
observe the crushed strokes of colour
where the angels of destruction will pass over
blood for destruction
blue for forgiveness
black for salvation

touch the crumbling folds of peeling paint for luck
chant te deums and count ten stones for blessings
one for each finger of healing mercies
and in the circle where the people gather in hope
gather all their counts of thanks for each departed soul
for here in this circle there is no fear
for here in this circle there is only praise
for here in this circle pain is the gateway to peace

hold hands, hold hands with lighted candles
seek out scraps of broken skin wedged like torn cloth
between the borders of pain and peace
place six candles of hope to shine their way
hold the seventh in your palm and speak like Ezekiel
in this valley of tattered flesh over broken bones
tell the daughters of Jarius to go wash in the river of hope

for I, Bon Dieu says: "In your palms I hold them
I hold them dear to my heartbeat to my heart

For the innocence of their body is to my liking
And I will raise them up with me in my glory days
And death then shall have no dominion."

After the Quake

You say this is not the poem you want for the auguries
As you step carefully over the rubble of these stone diaries
Stolen from Les Trois Rivères that empty into Lac de Péligre
To build mansion defenses against us who carry the stones
But which now stand as our sudden departure tombstones
Those zoom lenses of the world love to capture for fun ratings
The dangerous hordes they caption in Plaine du Cul-de-Sac
We who seek the salt waters of healing from Etang Saumâtre
To heal our swollen tongues of bitterness
To wash our eternal hope of emptiness
But since as you seek meaning in the bitterness in your heart
To record the pain of those interned in these clods of red earth
You may one day write praise poems that celebrate their birth

After the Quake, Floods (Mami Cèlésté)

We trod our way through sleuths of broken mud to Chabett Clearing
There we arraigned neatly our ornaments worshipping
We each entered the prayer circle of ashes, emerging
White lines covering our bodies and like skeletons, dancing
We chant the litany of loas thanking them for receiving
Those whose spirits had left so sudden at the earth's trembling
Thanking them for those who surprised at their separation from hope
Those who have stepped hugely into the ocean deeps without hope
Those carried on the shoulders of bulbous waters singing of rivers
Singing of these broken banks of Guayamouc and Massacre rivers
We had prayed they would ride in the blue boat rowed by she in red
To be cleansed in the Pedernales River before they rise as mist
Enter the mystery spaces of Montagnes Noires and then enlist
Visions of sea memories and prayers that hope can be fed

For Those Singed in Fear

This poem then is for all those singed in the silence of fear
Who over these three centuries refuse to surrender to grief!
Though seasoned ire grips and gnaws their larynxes of pain
Threatening to throttle their visions of hope without fear
It is for those who prune their pain to weave new dream baskets
To gather this scattered flesh among crushed bones and stones
To re-member the fractious spirits wandering among these Massifs
We have seen them at break of dawn or dusk carrying caskets
Circling Massif de la Salle, Massif la Hotte, Chaîne de la Mathieux
Looking for a drowning of their tears in the Libón or Artibonite
The desperate that tumble down from Montagnes du Trou d'Eau
With those who did not perish in the year of the death at Massacre River
Return to gaze once more where a cruel god had let them live, they quiver
And then they plunge their sacrifice of heads upon the rocks below

A Voice Cries on the Mountain Top

A voice rose in the cold morning above these cracked mountains
"Beware of the season of planting," it cried, "beware the season of planting
The world again will converge at your gates with gourds of promises
In the night of your lamentation because your children are no more
Determined once again they will come to banish the dreams of Macandal
They are already here as I speak, carrying Boukman's severed head
Dragging L'Ouverture away from the window he had opened in your souls
They will come from many places, but fear more those from Naples
They will come with a mandate: 'Remember', they will be told in braille
'Your duty is to bring peace to a savage place with unruly urges
'Your mandate: pacify; ideology: Negrophobia; action: extermination
'Not by bloodletting but by water polluting for their starving guts'
They will come with excremental vision and inject death by cholera
For they will say, better that many die than few be disgraced
Oh my Aiyiti! When again will my children laugh in innocent dreams?"

While listening to Dr Jack Coulehan read poems about his patients

English Department, UPR October 11, 2012

Rapture of the Six-Hundred-Pound Man

You too my six-hundred-pound Jamaican-American brother
Have found your way in your passing among the pages of poets
For unlike those others who would crunch "Dr Big Nose" into stench
Who without a body but strong in bicep power could throw an uppercut
Yet found themselves strapped in wheelchairs of anger and despair
You who without "Lillian's" glass eye of clearer visions
Yet walked your way through the fire that burns the spine

Gari ba nye! (Well done!)

You my six-hundred-pound brother etherized upon two beds
In these white and silent halls with whispers and moving wheels
Suspended with IV tubes and giant needles that feed on your pain
The dream of every intern anxious to see the colour of sickness
As they crawl over your body like millipedes in astonishment
Looking at their charts detailing the colour of disease
Yet with those eyes you smiled with grace at their irreverence

Jaang yo! (Well done!)

I feel their gloved fingers poking your every crevice spinning you around
Their professors monitoring their every move that confirms their theory
That sickness, dying, and death have colours of choice
But you my six-hundred-pound brother with no stars in your insides
And yet you like "Antonio" welcomed pneumonia as your ticket home
Though you never kissed the hands that poked and strung you up
In this chamber where you became a piece of wonder for all to see

E mo yeng! (Well done!)

You my six hundred pounds brother from the shadows of Blue Mountains
You my six-hundred-pound brother from the foothills of Cockpit Country
You my six-foot six-hundred-pound brother from the shadow of Twin Sisters
On that midnight of your rapture we wept for joy and prayed also
That ours too will happen, suddenly leaving smile wrinkles on our faces
As we ride the waves of our triple seas back to Maroon Country
Where Nanny awaits to give birth to us while chanting Sankofa, Sankofa

Gari ba nye!

My six-hundred-pound brother uncontainable by "Man Mountain Dean"
You longed for the free spaces where your birth stone is buried
Not to be cured by six prescriptions from a "Medicine Stone"
Obtained on "a cold June day near Wounded Knee" and a "sprig of shage"
I am the unashamed "Haitian cab driver on the Medical run"
Bringing Celia our sister with her potted plant of life to your bedside
Announcing that in your going is our personal redemption

Jaang yo!

So you see, my six-hundred pounds Jamaican brother dying in America
We may be heartbroken at your rapture but we are heart-emboldened
To know that the Sankofa bird has carried you above raging waters
To where you can tell your stories of migration to those to come
In the nine-nights of our memory where you ride those with vision
And give us strength each year on ancestral remembrances days
Across this island of hopes deferred yet reborn in your passing

Praise be!

Hear then my six-hundred-pound for pound brother with smiling teeth
That we sit here in the circle of tears with lighted candles of peace
Ancestral drums and maracas calming our turbulent desires
Your name in the circle of stone angels that guard our lives at night
Your spirit a cloak of strength in these depressions of faith
As we walk through the gathering darkness you light the paths of love
Mysterious waterways to our Caribbean guarded by six-hundred-
pound bodies

Praise be!

Watching slides of scars while Jim Ferris performs a poem about scars

What are scars worth?
Scars are ugly, scars are mean
Scars are disgusting on the skin
Scars are scary but sublime
Scars are tough, scars are cool
Scars will make you understand
Scars will ruin your perfect life
Scars unveil your body's lies
Scars complete your humanity

So my title poem will begin with a grated knee
My poem will echo the sound from a cleft on the hunches
My poem will be a shadow of a dry river of blood
Overhanging the knee cap protruding like a swollen testicle
My poem will be a hanging membrane like an unwanted earlobe

This poem definitely will be the limb petered out
Like the beak of a starved vulture or stork
Pointing earthward in supplication to the knife of surgeons
My poem will be a badly restored mashed-up sawn cartilage
My poem will be a scar against poetry
Blobs of unfinished flesh rising like dough
Like a cowboy in a bandit's sombrero
The head a history of the scalpels passing slice

My poem must become if I dare the shadowy cleaver
It will not discriminate between fresh flesh and rotten meat
It only knows its religion of power is to cleave
And leave gullies of deboned flesh or de-fleshed bones
But remains free of memory except a shining glint

At its performance of excellence across the abdomen
Seeking blood sacrifice to save lives of those who dare
To bow before it in prayerful mood

My poem will reveal the secrets shrouded behind caftans
My poem will lift up silky robes and display the covered shame
Of sutured stories beyond recognition and remorse
My poem will uncap foreheads to proclaim testimonies
Of slashes of manhood in the dark lanes of mean streets
And the unfinished slash across the esophagus and neck
What bravery to have defeated these other knives in a fight!
And walked to bloody manhood's fame
My poem will wail behind me as I remove my shirt
To reveal dry streams of corrugated flesh
What stories crisscross this broad and squishy back
My poem will not reveal, for it came too late to know
Do not turn away in disgust or fear or panic
This back is not your back but mine alone
I only wish to share the richness of its history
With the poverty of experience of your immaculate back

Thus this poem will rise to new low heights in awe of its power
Here then, see this exotic and refined scar
An under a great worm wriggling along the epidermis
Everyone except you praise the tombstones of pacesetters
No one praises the artificial heartbeat that keeps me alive
Un-remembering the chainsaw purring through the breastplate
Here touch it; squeeze the beauty of its squishiness
Soft, smooth, jelly feeling like yogurt or custard

This scar on my left arm is like a poem yet to be read
It is an aesthetic of a veritable millipede slapped stuck
On these unpronounced biceps
Scares the real ones when they smell it
But oh the best is a 3D carved on my right hand

A half-done egg in a skillet still warm in melted butter
I admire it daily to satisfy my need for poached eggs
It turns the stomachs of others and I feel powerful

Oh but for a poem of scars to celebrate their victory
For scars are not evil but stories of conquest of evil
The skin without scars is not yet born
For we all have scars of separation from our mothers
Scars you make me feel alive and you deserve praise.
All hail to the scars of human history and the body collective.
Amen to scars in Caribbean histories limping to St Croix . . .

Christiansted, St Croix

Navigating Christiansted, St Croix
Arriving in St Croix
As a neophyte of learning
You must take a taxi van
And head fast for Christiansted
There to your right
The old Moravian stands guard
Over the entrance to Christiansted
As St John's Episcopal falls in ruins
Empty pews tell of the new beginnings
In the embrace of disgrace

Stop at Time Square and take a sip of water
Turn right and climb through the Free Guts
See, this is where the bold and the free of Africa
Those followers of Buddoe and Mary
Survived the whip lash and hurricane floods

If you must eat in the heat of midday sun
Carry your groaning tummy to Singh's Chop Bar
There you can fill your sack of desires
With tasty rotis and curried goats
Fish, conch, shrimp, and chicken too

On top of Hill Street and Queen Street
By Coffe's Great House
You must gaze in wonder
At the spectacle of the Gallows
Where the ghosts of drowned Africans
Who dared to raise a fist against their chains
Breeze through the white sails of yachts
Or shout the word *Uhuru*
Beside bloodstained roofs
Guarded by mustard-coloured Fort Christiansvaern

Arriving beside the fort
The welcome inscription reads:
Fort Christiansvearn 1749
This fort played a vital role
In Christiansted's international trade
Built to protect the city from pirates
Built to prevent the slaves from insurrections
Built to protect the king's men from privateers

Beside it nothing else speaks to you
Except the tree that leans in defiance
This tree proudly labeled The Whipping Tree
The bust of David Hamilton Jackson 1884-1946
The Black Moses as if Moses of Egypt was white
Leading his people away from the tree

Here at Salt River Bay
Columbus soaks his rot-foot toes
His commanders crouch whispering
Murmuring against the great man
Planning to wash their swords
In the tropical blood of Caribs
At Cabode las Fletches
While they, innocent, play their ball game

This yellow walled Limpricht Port
Refuses to welcome strangers like me
For the doors to memory long ago were buried
In the rushing floods of the guts
And the mixed screams of flesh under the whip
For in 1917 he lowered the flag of the Danes
And the Star Spangled Banner rang through
The hollow curves of the surrounding hills
Merging with calypso at Rainbow Beach

Rainbow Beach, St Croix

Weaving my way
Through half-nude flesh
Bikini this and bikini that
Against leftover bellies
Over struggling swimsuits
Sand dirty like dirt
The worshippers dig in
But only the kids float
Above the surfless waves

You can easily tell
The children sport Mohawks
Riding poles on the sand
Respond to these garbled voices
Slurping joy from bottles
Eating mountains of cotton candy
Waiting for the end-of-year performance

End-of-Year Performance Night

Claude O Markoe School, St Croix May 2009

The sight of *akenten*
The sound of the *longo*
The *maracas* and the *kongas*
All testify to the squeals of pleasure awaited
Among the kids with expectant hearts

The drums drum their drum message
Ghosts of Taino and Dagaaba
Rise to the call of ritual
Steal through the rafters
Settle among the crowd

The living from every island in this horizon
The living shadows from distant continents
Gaze into the distance of the stage
And the skin drums call to steel drums
The conch calls to buffalo horn
To the deep blue seas
Rising above mountain tops
Rushing east to arrive west of everywhere

The ancestors mingle with the descendants
The descendants mix with the invaders
The invaders mix with the invited
Unheard music moves the stilted feet
Of these *Mokko-jumbos*
They dance tied to yellow cloths

A ladder leans to the left
Toward one on the back wall
Rise through the roof

I see a crowd clad in white
Moving up and down the ladder
Those who died to form this identity
Those that died to kill this identity
Those that did nothing for this identity
Those that stole from this identity
These that await consolidated identity
All in vain are appointed a time to wait
For to the left of the ladder
St Croix flag hangs limp in the still wind
To the center a star- banner flag flutters violently where there is no wind
Somewhere in a corner
A Danish white and blue cloth peeps
For everywhere the signal reads
Might is right
Wealth is right
The language of identity is monolingual

After dedicated rituals
To god hung on a tree
The drums call:
They call to *Atabey*
The drums call:
They call to *Oludumare*
They call: they call Odumankuma
They call: they call to Kala and Wilaa
They chant Ra, Ra, and Osiris Rising
There is silence.

The silence is broken
Kindergartens kindle their pride
Rearrange like sea waves
The letters: A E I O U

American English I Owe You
Spoken in tongues of the true North
Proclaimed in accents of the true West
As Cruzan escapes the slaughter of her voice
We all cheer and shriek approval

Then lumber up the steps
First and second graders
On their lips hang the words:
"Little Boy Blue"

I question my memory
What can little kinders do
Garrisoned in knowledge factories
Carrying tutorial board games
To the right or to the left
While a little black boy
Is forced to sleep in the center?

I get my response from 2/3 graders
"I can Chant"
"I can Chant"
They yell in mixed voices
Sporting the ditto: "I am drug free"
The little guy in the middle
Stamps to the unheard rhythm
Steals the movement of the body
Guided by unseen hands

We shall not be outdone
Sings a duet in
"Farewell my friend, Adios"
I felt the end is come
But this merely preludes

What is christened "Danza Africana"
My jaw drops
Clangs noisily on the metal table
Which one someone asks
I would like to know
In this forest of Diaspora dreams
Memories are mangled and minced
Into what can be selected
What can be invented?
But the girls do move well
The singing astonishes me in its particularity

"Wa wako sink la I ko"
Choreographed repetition
Memorized inventions for the neophytes
Of ancestral logic

"Mango Man" is next in line
A dance for mama
A jig for papa
As the curtain opens again
Each child holds a knee
Each child holds a waist
Like their tired parents
While the tape recorder gurgles out some music
The spirits intervene
There is no music from this thing from Japan
The curtain closes

If Mango Man could not sing in Japanese
Beyonce's "All the Single Ladies" refused to chorus
For the bewildered crowd
A debate rages below the stairs
For the "Stay in School" poem
The grade fivers maintain their cool

They refuse to leave school
They assert their rule
In this moment of spooks

For an instant
White-and-yellow clad damsels
Move onto the stage
Cutting through the food aromas
So close to me to my right
My stomach growls
Yet I must be still
To see the discipline of duplicated movements
Retrieved from cell memory
Resurrecting what had been buried
Below the rock of impalement
Where to drum was to die
Here they are living the dance of the Guinea coast
The song of evening
Breaks through the voices
I do not know the words
I do not know their smells
But like worship calls
All hands fling in unison
Their white kerchiefs
Rise from yellow-draped arms
And solo dancers take center stage
To the call of ancestral gods
Of this place and other places
To the call of present gods
Of this place and other places
As we sip coke through straws and applaud
Is this the identity?

In the plaza of apish pleasure

We grind and wind to reggae-ton
Like atrophied runners in a marathon
The smell of perfumed sweat
Rises to the zest of life

Admiring a private collection in St Croix

The road to this house on a hilltop is graced with danger
But our bus makes it up real slow with lots of groans
We are welcomed warmly into the large hall of the family
After some pleasantries, we are escorted into a family museum
My companions stare in absolute amazement
At the vast array of displayed artifacts in one man's possession
On an island where much is forgotten or denied

I have come because I want to be angry at history
As I predicted the first items I perceive are Taino tools
The manorial lord explains about their use to us
He must have been there when these things were made
I am *flabberwhelmed* with these Taino figurines
Their stone and marble carvings encased in glass prisons
Together with imprisoned souls from San Domingue

Lines criss-crossing these archipelagoes are patterned
Here two lined faces in this clay boat
They call this, we are told, Bocachica typography
Bocachicas according to conquistador calculations
Are believed to be the highest developed Taino art
There is uncertainty of course in manufactured facts
As our creative interpreters throw sea water on the theory

We enter into another cage of Carib warfare
Crude blunt stone axe heads meant for clubbing
More than for scalping iron-helmeted heads of Europeans
More than for resisting slaughter from razor-edged swords
I look in vain for those from the Middle Passage
I must wait for a journey to Whims Museum
To read the litany of names I have known from home

Here, see, look well in this collection
I also possess the bust of Sir Henry Morgan

Miniaturized, bought in Belgium through Martinique
I must say. I am lucky to be the only man in St Croix
To boast of such a bust of the famous pirate
On the bookshelf to the left is a letter
From Colonel Green to Alexander Hamilton to Washington
Reporting of the French plot to sell St Croix to the Spanish
They could only go so far we are told
The gunpowder that left Christiansted
Docking at the bay of Delaware
Could only blow up the unwary British
And you must know, I am related to the French Governor
Sir Phillipe de Poincy through William Peebles and Anne Jones
So you are looking at royalty of an ancient line

Oh but you must see my collection of Danish swords
Mark these stabbing knives good now for opening mail
I forgot to mention I also have on the Crucian side
My African past of a slave grandfather
Now displaced on a glass table naked to your glances
But of the children born on plantations
That history is controlled into silence

But as you can see behind this bookcase
Between the books of the Byzantine Empire
And the empires of Matilda and Mary queen of Scots
There sits the severed head of an African queen
Said to lead the slaves to revolt against the masters
other heads of other Africans rise on poles
outside the city gates as lessons for the foolish

Buddhoe's fingers shiver over the machete's edge
Turn over the leaves that ensure his people's slavery
Bidrag the Beskrivelse over St Croix
Over St Thomas, Over St John, over Tortola.
1793.

St Croix: the Haunts of Castle Coakley, I

I walked over to the shed
where two old Cruzians shared a rum
under the shade of the neem
enquired about the road to Castle Coakley
and in soft Cruzian, they spoke:

"just keep pushing forward
soon you will find ancient footprints
set by those who marched there
to whip lash and chain fire
broken shoulders on hot boulders."

then in soft echoes a gargled laughter escaped their lips
I walked on wondering

at last I rounded a bend
I climbed the hill of history
where once stood a house of power
but all that remains to be seen
are these renegade stones
sprawled dejected everywhere
while the revenge of cane
shoots through broken chimneys
in these rusty plantation boilers

is standing I standing quiet quiet
magnified by chants of crickets
whistling to dance of noon heat
under a dying sea grape:

"where once the proud Dane from Copenhagen
where once the proud French from Paris

where once the proud Spaniard from Andalucía
where once the proud British from London

defeated their fear of beauty in a bottle of rum
boasted in powers of their tribes
backed by powder and canon ball
only iguanas now parade in yellow bandanas
claiming territory in pitched battles of the tail!"

so is walking I walking sofly sofly
is looking I looking new dreams
come rise from ancestral quarters
where once fungi and breadfruit
sustained the hope of freedom
sustained the salvation promised
waves a torn flag in an afternoon breeze

near these ruins of Great Houses
no image of Buddhoe rises
no memory of the slave boy
waving the Union Jack
in the march on Frederiksted
proclaiming on that July noon
"any flag wid don do for get awa fridom"
as Von Schoeton bowed.

St Croix: the Haunts of Castle Coakley, II

I misjudge my paper titles
obtained from foreign lands of the West
where knowledge is manufactured

I misjudges my name
in the illusion of my passport
that I am the ananse circulated in their lore
carrying my gourd of truths from Ghana
in these US Virgins of Caribbean islands
thus walking in a daze of disillusion
I round the bend of sanity
stop. recall the read signs
and listen to the litany of names:

St Alba, St Lucia, St Martin/Saint Marten
St Bart, St John, St Croix
St Kitts, Sainte Domingue
St Vincent, St Eustacio among others

I say my angelus
perhaps these names, oh so saintly!
may become my crucifixion, my absolution
where to hang in silence, on the left side of a cross
before unseeing eyes of ancestors sacrificed
to placate these names of Christendom
will be my redemption, my condemnation
I embrace my sizzling illusion

Notice Inside Whims Museum, St Croix

"1770 Ano Dominum; Wanted: Woman named Hetty!"

from Patrick M'Donough

"Be ye all informed that I
Johannes offers a handsome reward
To any and sundry who may
At any time and place or clime capture, my property
Kidnap or arrest and return to me, my property
A woman named Hetty, my property
A likely BLACK NEGRO woman, my property
Named Hetty, a washer woman, my property
Ironer and middle aged woman, my property
A grinder and cleaner woman, my property
She carried away with her my property
In the form of a child she bore for me, my property
A little black child about four years of age, my property
Named Mary."
1770 of our Lord.

So we set out in heady haste in search of Hetty, his property
You and I formerly also the properties of others
Kindred spirits at midnight wandering on the loose
Plotting how to persuade these ancient knees
To carry us up the Beston Hill of hidden caves
Where La Grange rises above blue smoke

We trudge like confused footmen to the lord's command
Begin our march through darkness and shifting shadows
Through rustling cinnamon branches that whisper secrets
Only people like Hetty and Mary could understand
Knowing we are doomed in our treachery
Un-hoping for any miracle of salvation
We march through foliage in this night of our need

We march on believing if we can survive
The sudden ghost behind neems on Lover's Lane
We would reach Sunny Isle Plaza for a rest
Thus emboldened by our fear of shadows
Hiding from manic cars to mimic men with machetes
We zigzag forward like zombies seeking freedom ways

Suddenly a taxi stops ahead of us
Our hearts begin to race to our mouths
A voice cracks the silent night air
"Boys you want a lift somewhere
We go to Beston Hill to Beston Hill"
Inside the taxi, the radio wails a Marley song:
"War in a Babylon, Tribal war in a Babylon!"
An uprising song on Queen Mary's Highway
For we whose minds are shielded by the white mask

But in our relief of forgetting so soon what it is to be chained
Marley's wailing reminds us of that fiery day in St Croix
When Mary, daughter of Hetty with fire in her hair
That Crucian Boudacia come from outside with fire in her eyes
Marched like an erupted volcano lighting her path
Purifying cane fields between Frederiksted and Christiansted
Where now the temples of academic pomposity stand
Built to worship the 3Rs of new enchaining

We forget our mission and at Beston Hill Medical Facilities
We seek a healing for our sins of forgetting
We two defeated kings of Isla del Encanto
Dismount, chant praise and glory up La Grange
Chant Fire in a Babylon through cinnamon trees.

Boarding to St Martin

at the gangway in Pearson Airport
to flight 5032
bound for St Maarten
bonded by dual occupation
bonded by multiple disinheritance
bonded by quilts of lamentations
a flight attendant hands me a magazine
colourful in name and feel
it reads: destination!   I ponder. To where?
it tempts: discovery!   I yield. To what?
it promises: escape!   I wonder: to/from
which five Ws?

but only I worry about the meaning inscribed on gloss
but only I think of no answers
of what escape destination
can discover for me in this homecoming to St Martin

I crawl into the plane's belly cramp my frame into a seat
strapped firm, I relax

Arriving in St Maarten / Martin

I look down from on high the B767
catch glimpses of ghosts of ancient ships
retching their black human cargo
upon this salt saturated soil
but now abandoned schooners
and livid cruise ships litter the bays
emptying steamy and desperate white souls
searching for life in these new Great Houses
imported casinos, hotels and nudist beaches
licensed plantations of pure pleasure
I am lured by their lurid appeals
I pay homage to the echoes of sorrow
rising from the overcrowded avenues
in tandem with ancestral grieving on faces

I must remember this to myself
these illusions of discovery
these new castles of escape
guarding the seacoasts of these Saints Marteens
stand on plantations of bones and blood
stand on graves of the unsung
where some ancestor made a final call
where an ancestress made a final call
and they still call to me across the depths of memory

I must remember this to myself
that here, there, and everywhere
in the dew-bathed morning
farmers of St Maarten
fishermen of Saint Martin
met at those salt ponds
where the salt reapers kept vigil at hope's end
at the going of the salt ponds.

Dreams in St Maarten / St Martin

the salt ponds are gone
the salt ponds are gone
wails a cracked voice
atop Pic Paradis at dusk

we whose ancestors' sweat sweetened these bitter lands
we turn in our couches of Xeroxed comfort
and shiver at these notions of borrowed boom
or relax in shivers of notions of borrowed doom
we sip sip through silent straws
multicoloured liquids of perdition
chaining our tomorrows
to our desires to forget

• o o o o o

the salt ponds are gone
the salt ponds are gone
nothing else remains
nothing else promises

the voice roles from mountain crest to mountain crest
taken up by birdsong
as they fly from tree top to tree top

from Pond Blanche
I look at the Keys /to what I ask?
guiding the various bays
where sex reapers flaunt their wares
and from yacht deck to Cruiser deck
sun-seekers flap white sails across the three seas
to sun-baked Saint Maarten/St Martin
to prostrate before a white sun on white sands

XXXXXXXXXXXXXXXXXXXXXXX

I clamber up King Hill
like an exiled king without hope
ponder on the new forts of power
erected by wielders of dollars
I see canons point in menace landward
toward Ebenezer and Philipsburg
toward St Peters and Marigot
baracoons afloat on crushed bones
and I ask:

???????????????????????????

is that a call I hear from Mt William
re-member re-member re-member it whispers
re-member dwellers of La Savanne
re-member dreamers of Grande Case
re-member survivors of Colombiere
re-member squatters at Cripple Gate
re-member strollers at Rambaud
of the ghosts at fore day morning
marching to Concordia Pass when the drum called out their names
of those who would not die the cruel death
of the sweetness of treacle or harshness of rum

I hear echoes from the ancient conch
from the shadows of Marigot Hill
I descend to the Lowlands
to search in these sands of time
traces of warrior steps
and await their coming chills
but only the hawks of pleasure swoop down

dropping scavengers of the sun
into these new bastilles of consumption
the saxophones of ease blur the night air
beckons nudists from every clime
to Naked Bay Hill and Sucker Garden
to where Pointe de Bluff rises and Plateau Red Rock converge

yet I do not despair in my dreams
for in this tumult of painful desires
echoes of deliverance tales may yet resound
for the children of Sekou of Mali
for the children of Kumbey of Ghana
for the children of Gao of Songhai
for the children of the Manlarla of Dagao
may yet hear the call to redemption
and heal those who care to reclaim their names
even on these dry abandoned ponds
so that over the children of life
death shall have no dominion

I. Saint Martin

And death shall have no dominion
death already rules the emptiness!

death dances beneath our seas of memories
conducts its rituals of terror
injects its ecstasies of now
into our dream-gourds of forgetting

Césaire saw it all
in his delirium of truths
"death expires in a white pool/of silence"
and the white horseman
rallies the daemons of justice
rallies daemons of despair
from the shadows of these archipelagos
beneath
beneath these rising concrete/stell
conquering all light in smoke riddles
following hunger's strides
and the armies of greed

but death shall have no dominion
the banner burnished
against the hallowed sun
death shall have
death shall have
death shall have no dominion
sniveling in the bowels
of we who squat in these bays of pirates

who run through hurricanes
"these paths without memory" (Césaire)

memorials buried on wind veins
ripple beneath turbulent waves
for our words alone
i say, our words alone
will not be our stories' ending
but if you gaze with shut-eye
you will hear the gurgle of their laughter
you will glimpse the glint of their winks
you will catch refracted signs
in the i-maging of silence
with no reason
with no intuition
with treasure chest of doubts

for we who perch on bayonet dreams
have no more nightmares to offer
only a sealed gourd of dread seeds
that seek black soil among granite
swinging among these cataracts
of Africa, Europe, America
these archipelagos of hope

II. Saint Martin

Night. Moon. Light. Mosquitoes. Men.
shadows glide and spy on us
as the house of Shujah
leaps sudden above the cliff
massive over the edge
of this bramble-held ravine
calls across voids to Ghana
silence

there beneath the starry nights
we five sit chanting against despair
fearing too loud a spell
could startle the ghosts of ancestral pasts
cause us to relive the horrors of their pasts
so there we sit
words heavy on our lips
unable to drop and splatter
on this divided rock of agony
named San Maarten/Saint Martin
where Lasana roams like The Baptist
gathering names of the fallen
putting flesh on the bones
scattered above "reclaimed lands" from salt ponds
where casinos now rise to meet the desires of tourists

the question: Who and what are we?
"A most worthy question!" (Césaire)

but how to respond without a language of love?
but how to ride the breeze of ancient violence?
a night cricket whistles in tune an answer:

ask not "who and what are we" a most unworthy question
ask: who and what are they
that in anxiety valley
forget that self, themselves
see only shades
ask: because we are therefore we think
therefore we are not?
who can say a thing is
therefore the thing is not?
a most undernourished proposition
yet the philosophy of en-light-en-ment
drowns the philosophy of truth

in the moonlit night of our present
looking beyond Marigot Hill
Anguilla sprawls, beyond and beyond to where
between lies a silence of connections
leaps from hill top to valley belly
skating on flood waters
heads for mountain top
where fire rises to embrace itself
and lies lie smoldering
as dying embers of truth
scatter around the dawn of my dying

Random Whispers in Kibuli Country: The Commonwealth of Dominica

where an ancient woman sleeps
the welcome sign reads: THIS IS KIBULI COUNTRY
I wonder who is Kibuli? I wonder what is Kibuli?

we pass close to a green kiosk
perched dangerously on the hillside

everywhere green bottles sprawl

dripping their last contents

of what once was Kibuli?

a beer, I learn from the taxi driver.

Touring Kibuli Country
I, Dominica

the conference is over
the gurus of knowledge are ecstatic
they have once again proved
that the annual ritual of words
of gathering to slap each other's backs
to see who could shout bigger jargon
is what their calling dictates
those that need to put a name to the face of the land
stay on to discover what the natives do not know
so they stay and hire local porters
to show them the contours of the land

I am one of the fortunate:
yet my task is to script
the journeys of land-discovery
the adventures of self-uncovery
so into the bus we go:

I will name the places here:
the journey begins at Landslide Mountain
our land cruiser zigzags along narrow paths
past walls of stone mastiffs
that loom above us ready to crush us
but held at bay by flimsy-dressed wozo weeds
that line and dance by sudden descents
onto rocky altars of gloomy boulders
where angry waters bubble and wait
to receive the sacrifice of rude tourists

somewhere to our right
a signboard reads out to us:
Welcome to Screw Spa

my Catholic spirit shudders
at this boldfaced invitation to sin
but there she stands, shameless
surrounded by her siblings:
Irie Man Screw and Entrance Screw

beside them rise misty steams
sent by secret ponds and caves
to scout for we degenerates
to drag down the disparate
to sulfuric purification
the names of these dragons of health include:
Dragon's Moth for dragon's mouth
Boiling steam Cave and Sulphur Spring
Stem Spring and Steam Geiger
these and those beyond memory
croon their seductiveness to the instant line-up
of neophytes tired of innocence in closed spaces
they disappear one by one
into the vapish wilderness of vapor
or to the warm suction of hot ponds

but beware dream seeker of eternal youth
at these ponds you cannot leave behind
your garment of age
beyond Paprilote Wilderness Resort
no battles can be fought
no hair can be brushed
no food can be brought
no cooling aid allowed
where the arrows of steam
pierce the skin of the wanderer

Touring Kibuli Country
II, Dominica

Everywhere Kibuli lubricates
the thirsty throats of wanderers

at the brows of mountains
white goats graze endlessly
where fresh-water springs
burst through mountain hides
we quench our cinnamon thirsts

we alight to rest at Cocoa Cottage
signs of earlier pilgrims to Trafalgar Falls
are seen in the debris of take-out lunch boxes
that line the way through Chirga Lillies and lemon grass

toward steam-bathed Lilly Valley Complex
Glocho Falls roars away from Easy Lizzy plants
and green dasheen dash us their succulent leaves
as we make our way toward Trafalgar Falls
in fearful silence of expectations

toward us hot breezes rush to meet us head-on
as we clamber through narrow slippery slopes
beneath ominous sentries of bamboo
beneath silent whispers of ancient elms
we trudge like maroons returning home
leading newly freed ancestors to life

Trafalgar Falls, Dominica

at the foot of Trafalgar Falls   a lone tree stands defiant
among broken boulders
daring these mountain shadows
giving sanctuary to homeless plants
where no root-folds are seen
all around it steam vapors
from entombed volcanoes
a warning sign belches:

this river enjoys suffering
from constant flash floods
so swimming is at your peril
to those not in ancestral mantels
nor in tune to the chant words
of the Caribs and the Maroons

through the mists of Trafalgar Falls
the sun dances uncertainly to the multirhythm
of hidden rivers above
and confused rivers below

the group moves along, cautiously
hugging the moss-clothed stones
but one whose ancestors had docked at Goree to purchase flesh
now stands like a new Columbus gazing in glee at his history
bares a chest weighed down by talismans seized from
Mandingo captives
to gaze and perchance to see back into time and distance
the ranges of the Futa Toro and the Futa Jallon
to claim his ancestors' global grasp of lands

The sign at Trafalgar Falls, Dominica

for Dianne Ursulin and her mother

the water has taken its first victim
a camera drops, drowning half way
in a tiny nook of a small creek
it is rescued but it no longer clicks
the horror!
for the spirits here must claim their very own
this daughter of Martinique in the dense woods of Dominica

maybe Christophine calls to her
from the Wide Sargasso Sea
through these waterfalls

she is silent
wondering why she must be chosen
But as a daughter out of Kumba
she absorbs it all in silent meditation
misunderstanding neighbors glare, impatient
that this stealer of our shadows
made to limit the voices of the unseen
made to swallow those presences
should be swallowed in its taking
and drown in its reflection by Mami Wata

later I learn that this contraption
belongs to a protective mother over the bridge
awaiting the return of a wandering daughter
and in her vision she intervenes with just a word
blows the camera down into the shallow water
to save her daughter from the call of the deeps below
where Trafalgar Falls to join the Sene
where Trafalgar Falls to merge with the Volta

Journey to Melville Hall Airport, Dominica

La Flamboyant sits dozing in sleepy Roseau
cars zigzag over cracked roads and pavements
gutters, broken, ooze green moss and blackish water
there the journey of departures begins
and meets me at St James Guest House

I board the minivan taxi
carrying abandoned gurus of knowledge
the driver is a gentleman in all proportions
I take the front seat beside him
puffed up like a fallen Prospero
sailing to Sycorax cove

soon a canefield pops up round a curve
but no more canes grow here
no treacle is squeezed out here
the sugar mill where a Macandal lost a hand
gazes sadly across the empty sea
by a dead discotheque
where the young and the aged went to forget

now it stands defeated
sans memory sans spirits sans story
dark, damp, dreary and weary
taken over by wild cane

Massacre:
(For those whose voices cry for obelisks of remembrances)

a fitting name for Black Atlantic places
how the name recalls its stories
this is my third ride through her arterial roads
at least some local artist
thinks it is about tomorrow
and painted these scenes of history:

see. here to your right
African ancestors cutting cane in canefield

there as in the Middle Passage
Africans merge with Caribs in pain

there in red uniforms French invaders grin
as a British trooper bayonets
a kneeling Chief Warner on the neck
driving the steel point through his chest
while other troopers applaud

all around the dead bodies of the innocent:
baby bodies. woman bodies. man bodies. many bodies.
all sacrifices to appease the hate
of an English son for a British father
who denied him the throne of Dominica

what crime did the Caribs commit
against the envious sons of Albion and of Gaul
they who welcomed them and gave them peace
only wanted to share their land with the foreigner

but they died, the Caribs died
they died so we might know death
death by whip lash
death of our tongue
death of our culture
death of self to self

so here we stand
nodding our heads
failing in comprehension
unwilling to understand
afraid to shed tears for the dead

whose presences tickle our dreams
for this was not the only massacre
all over the Antilles peaks
massacres await still to be mourned
whose voices cry for an obelisk of remembrance

it is our turn to mourn
for the massacres of our dreams
by these voices from beyond death
shouting by the wayside in our journeys
showing us the routes to Belles

Belles Village

showing us the routes to Belles
is a tedious job without memory
says our guide in a weary voice
except Gleau Gonmieres
who gave us the canoe
to traverse these 365 rivers
of sulfur fresh-water lakes
fish above these smoky mountains
Canada had ventured in here
promising rapid development
yet yearning to rape these forests
killing what they did not understand
they left just as Rochester had left
now we dig out their footprints
in these dangerous underwater bridges
where flood waters sweep all to sea

along the narrow gorge
dreamy Bois Hill descends to take a sip
from the cool rushing waters of Dieu Bois River
as Jacko and Sisserou confide
watching the falls thunder
through Stonefield and Sultan Estate
toward La You Valley and Elephant Ears

somewhere Grande Souffrier awaits Morne Aux Diables
Morne Diablotins conjures Morne Trois Pitons
Wotten Waven welcomes the call of Micotin
Morne Anglais reaches out to Watt Mountain
at Morne Plat Pays Volcanic Complex
all converging to conspire in the Valley of Desolation
to awaken the larva goddess
to renew her land with vigor
as we surge toward Concorde

Concorde, Dominica

Busy Lizzy owns this landscape
setting lemon grass as bush tea
to counter the menace of Dengue
in these rocky volcanic hills
road signs testify to a bold question mark
?
answers, but there are no answers now
to questions of belonging or not belonging
or to the politics of Why? What? How? Who? and When?
I the silent stranger seal my lips and dream
about how the Kalingo Crap and Hall Rivers flow silently to
River Concorde
East to Carib Enclave West to Concorde
as the rain drives the foreigner
from the island into his silver bird of departures

Arriving in Melville Airport, Dominica

closing in on Melville Airport
we run through Marigot land
here the people hang out
perched on broken steps
paying homage to thundering Sangmweni from across the Atlantic
sending arrows of rain as messengers he has not forgotten them

soon we enter Sam's Cutter
in the lilting houses lining along the narrow highway
the weary squat in weirs waiting for any news
from Monkey Hill Lions, Over Gutter, and The Bay
I do not know
but here in Melville Estate anything is possible
for the land dams the raging ocean
and the Atlantic lashes these shores
eating away the rocks of memories
as the airport emerges squat
in the shadows of towering mountains

Burning in Maroon Camp

I stand here sighing
leaning over the bridge
that straddles the Reseau River
wondering why the sea thirsts so much for fresh water

cars pass me by
under hot veranda shades people sip kibuli from bottles
as a Rasta elder strides along Babylon streets
nods an ancient prophetic recognition of beards
his bag and staff determines his strides of comfort
and I, whose praises he sings silently
am afraid to carry on like him

I turn to my compañeras
I learn that only the night before
the whole library of the Maroons
exploded in a smoke of domestic arson
set by one of their own lost to the rage of America
I recall Alexandria and Timbuktu and Djenne and Gao
and the architects of amnesias now called makers of civilization

what could they have given her
in that land of frozen breath
to turn her ovaries inside out and around
to set herself, her past, our future on fire like Antoinette

no answers save only a hasty idea:
those who burnt down Alexandria
and broke the nose of the Sphinx
and looted the pyramids
those children of Prospero who imprisoned Sycorax

and tried to steal from her son his humanity
have spawned across the Atlantic also
and have recruited new Ariels with white masks
to continue their rages of destruction
but fires of ire cannot dry out our memory of survival
soon flood waters of our love will snuff out these fires of hate
and only a sizzling silence of their hate will linger with them
where the seabed writes our history on its waves

De Profundi for Professor Joan Fayer

Joan Fayer, Joan Fayer
We call your name in Rio Piedras
But only the smells of silence respond

We chant your name in Philipsburg
But only the sighs of silence respond
For the ghost of Mrs Carmichael
Would not let you speak of Kromantin

We shout your name again and again
In the flooded plains of Cariacou
But only hurricane Lenny responds
To the dance of Shakespeare masks

We scrub the forest floors of Nieves
We look for forgotten footprints
Where you visioned Africa
In the language of her people

We dance on stilts after sundown
At the crossroads in St Croix
Awaiting your ululation of praise
But you are gone beyond the silent hills
To the rocky plains of Antigua

At the borders of Antigua
Our joyous spirits ride the waves
To bathe these volcanic rocks of departures
Toward Afro-French Guadeloupe

To Guadeloupe then we came with you

And looked across to sister Martinique
But somehow the bridge was beyond scope
And now you are gone beyond these clouds
To double-breasted St Lucia

Oh! Santa Lucia! Santa Lucia!
The convent nuns welcomed us
And morning after morning
We filed for Communion
Counting sunrises and rosary beads
As the Monsignor chanted de profundis

We marched on courting sundowns
We beat the dawning drums of youth
Headed for BVI Tortola
To awaken our dazed songs of expectations
You led the way, Joan, you led the way
But now you are silent

Joan Fayer, Joan
Fayer
A little of your laughter
For the sound of the unbeaten *pintin-pa*
Announces your dance name

We squatted at these watery edges
Beneath the eyes of El Yunke
Listening for the calming voice of Joan Fayer
She called us to the distant hills of Tobago

Yes. St Vincent and the Grenadines
Let me mention your names also
For Joan Fayer towered here among her peers
Speaking of Jaja of Opobo
Shedding his grief among the Caribs

Joan Fayer, we call your name in UPR
But only these soft rushes of shivers
Scatter our calloused fragments of memory
But only empty stillness holds our gazes
Across the sea islands of Puerto Rico

Joan Fayer, Joan Fayer
We ask: what is that rustling sound
We hear on the nights of 14 October?
Who is that walking so royally?
Up these stairs to Room 107
Where anxious faces await in vain?
It is Joan Fayer! It is Joan Fayer!
The sound of unbeaten pintin-pa
Announcing her dance names
Joan Fayer has become
The sound of the unbeaten pintin-pa
Announcing our dance names

Somewhere a weaverbird wails
Somewhere our souls engulfed in loss wail
We carry our hammers of pain
And seek to break the absence of memory
Joan Fayer you have become
The sound of the unbeaten pintin-pa
Announcing our names
Joan Fayer, grandaunt of this gathering
You are gone with a secret of hope
You have become the secret of sound

Through the incense of your love
Through the gates of paradise heights
The message drifts among our midst

Rises from heart valley to heart valley
Seeping through these concrete cracks

Our songs of sorrow echo
Echo in every basement
Ruffles the tender roots of knowing
And we carry our simmering pain
And we seek your smile in vain

Joan Fayer, just a memory of your smile
Just a memory of your soothing presence
For we sit twisted in these corridors of lament
Uncertain in the rituals of today's ceremonies
For all the rest will be silence

And the rest is silence
And the rest is silence
And the rest is silence

Joan Fayer Kuori Yelbie

Joan Fayer! Joan Fayer!
Fo zomeneng boala
Ba boalang kong vɛng yee
Ba boalang kong tang yee
Joan Fayer woo!
Ayi yeh woo!
Ayi ayi yeh woo aahii!

Joan Fayer! Joan Fayer!
Zing kyɛnli kyɛ wono
Zing boing kyɛwonaa zaa
Zing zom kyɛ wono yee
Ayiila woo
Ayi yeh woo!
Ayi ayi yeh woo aah!

Joan Fayer! Joan Fayer!
Karing mine pog-naah
Kareng kaaraa karema
Bang gang kyɛyel fii yee
Ayi laa woo
Ayi yeh woo!
Ayi ayi yeh woo pati!

Joan Fayer! Joan Fayer!
E kareng biiri hiineng
E kareng biiri hiine waana
Kareng biiri hiine sigre
Iri mogle ba
Ayi yeh woo!
Ayi ayi yeh woo aahii!

Joan Fayer! Joaan Fayer!
Kyin-kyarang la fo kuu
Kyin-kyanrang la vinle yee
Te konong te wiebo
Te kong bang tang
Ayi yeh woo!
Ayi ayi yeh woo pa!

Joan Fayer! Joan Fayer!
Dupey, ne McMurray ne Collins la kono
Sander neng Krasinsky
Alma neng Albuyeh
Lang kono wana
Ayi yeh woo!
Ayi ayi yeh woo aahii!

Joan Fayer! Joan fayer!
Acaria neng Pousada la kono
Rodriguez ba bayi
Lowell neng MacLeren
Lang kono waana
Ayi yeh woo!
Ayi ayi yeh woo pati!

Joan Fayer! Joan Fayer!
Nalini ne Bothwell ne Haydee la kono
Pedreira ne Yolanda
Conlan neng Rubiano
Lang kono waana
Ayi yeh woo!
Ayi ayi yeh woo aku!

Joan Fayer! Joan Fayer!
Stanchich ne Slagle la kono

Swope neng Gonzalez
Mervyn neng a Olsen
Lang kono waana
Ayi yeh woo!
Ayi ayi yeh woo aku!

Joan Fayer! Joan Fayer!
Weinraub neng a Julie la kono
Sharp neng Faraclas
Hurley neng Arbuckle
Lang kono waana
Ayi yeh woo!
Ayi ayi yeh woo aku!

Joan Fayer! Joan Fayer!
Greenberg neng Schnitzer la kono
Bernquist neng a Noel
Ba zaa la zing miine
Lang kono waana
Ayi yeh woo!
Ayi ayi ye woo aahii!

Joan Fayer! Joan Fayer!
Ester neng Joana ne Rosa
Anna neng a Sandra
Angel neng a Marcos
Lang kono waana
Ayi yeh woo!
Ayi ayi yeh woo ahii!

Joan Fayer! Joan Fayer!
Lebron neng O taaba la kono
Kong wa deɛ Joe Fayer
Kong wa deɛ Jane Fayer
Ayi laa woo!

Ayi yeh woo!
Ayi ayi yeh woo pati!

Joan Fayer! Joan Fayer!
E bidao Dannabang la boala
Boala kyɛ kono yee
Kono kyɛ boala yee
Puerto Rico puong
Ayi yeh woo!
Ayi ayi yeh woo aba!!

Dannabang Kuwabong is a Ghanaian Canadian born in Nanville in the Upper West Region of Ghana. He was educated in Ghana, Scotland, and Canada and teaches Caribbean literature at the University of Puerto Rico, San Juan. He has published four books: *Konga and other Dagaaba Folktales, Visions of Venom* (poetry), *Echoes from Dusty Rivers* (poetry), and *Caribbean Blues and Love's Genealogy* (poetry). Kuwabong's poetry adds a new dimension to the growing body of new voices that is beginning to expand and redefine Canadian literature.